W9-ADB-863

ENCOUNTERS WITH THE PAST

MEET THE VIKINGS

Alex Woolf

Gareth Stevens
PUBLISHING

Please visit our website, **www.garethstevens.com**. For a free color catalog of all our high-quality books, call toll free 1-800-542-2595 or fax 1-877-542-2596.

Woolf, Alex.
Meet the Vikings / by Alex Woolf.
p. cm. — (Encounters with the past)
Includes index.
ISBN 978-1-4824-0902-4 (pbk.)
ISBN 978-1-4824-0900-0 (6-pack)
ISBN 978-1-4824-0903-1 (library binding)
1. Vikings — Juvenile literature. 2. Civilization, Viking — Juvenile literature.
I. Woolf, Alex, 1964- II. Title.
DL65.W66 2015
948—d23

First Edition

Published in 2015 by
Gareth Stevens Publishing
111 East 14th Street, Suite 349
New York, NY 10003

Editors: Joe Harris and Nicola Barber
Design: Elaine Wilkinson
Cover design: Elaine Wilkinson

Cover pictures Shutterstock: house jps, archer De Visu, ship Danny Smythe, brooch Kachalkina Veronika.

Picture acknowledgements: Alamy: p18 Bildbroker.de; p20 Anders Blomqvist; p22 Ted Byrne; p24 Michele Boiero; p26 Richard Peel. The Bridgeman Art Library: p23 top Boltin Picture Library. Corbis p4 arm ring Heritage Images; p13 bottom Radius Images; p19 top Werner Forman; p25 bottom Carmen Redondo; p29 Werner Forman. iStockphoto: p15 top Sb-borg. Shutterstock: p4 background Khunaspix, inset top Charlie Edward, wallet Talip Cubukcu, coins Route66; pp5 and 28 De Visu; pp6-7 and 7 bottom De Visu; p6 Popova Valeriya; p7 top Danny Smythe; pp8-9 and title page De Visu, p8 Kachalkina Veronika; p9 top Celiafoto; pp10-11 Attila Jandi; p10 Radu Razvan; p11 top Kachalkina Veronika; p11 bottom Audrius Merfeldas; pp12-13 Tlorna; p12 Sergey Kamshylin; p13 top and contents Popova Valeriya; pp14-15 jps; p14 and title page De Visu; p15 bottom Rhimage; pp16-17 Can Erdem Satma; p16 Markgraf; p17 top Ckchiu; p17 bottom Zadiraka Evgenii; pp18-19 Worradirek; p19 bottom and title page De Visu; pp20-21 Attila Jandi; p21 top Popova Valeriya; p21 bottom Michal Lazor; pp22-3 Algol; p23 bottom Popova Valeriya; pp24-5 Wildnerdpix; pp25 and 28 Kachalkina Veronika; pp26-7 ajt; p27 top Harvepino; p27 bottom De Visu. Wikimedia Commons: p9 bottom WyrdLight.com.

Printed in the United States of America

CPSIA compliance information: Batch CS15GS: For further information contact Gareth Stevens, New York, New York at 1-800-542-2595.

Contents

Into the Past

You are visiting the city of York, England, with your family. Your parents have gone shopping, but you don't want to join them, so you're sitting on a bench by the River Ouse, texting your friends. Suddenly, right in front of you, a door appears. There are no walls around it – it's just a plain, wooden door.

People are walking right past the door – you seem to be the only one who can see it. For a moment, you sit, amazed. Then you put away your phone, stand up, and open the door. You step through and find yourself in a room with a stone floor and white walls. On a table in front of you is a pile of clothing, a leather pouch and some coins, and a parchment with the following words written on it:

▲ This silver Viking arm ring has dragon heads at either end. Arm rings were worn by Viking men and women to display their wealth.

Your Mission

You are about to visit the Viking settlement of Jorvik (York) in the year 1000CE. Your mission is to meet people and find out about their lives. The mission will last six hours.

Quickly, you choose some clothes from the pile on the table: a linen shirt, a tunic, trousers, and leather ankle boots. There's a silver arm ring, too. When you're dressed, you look up and notice that the scene through the open doorway is now very different. You take a deep breath and step outside. You find yourself on a busy quayside. People are loading and unloading wooden sailing ships. There are horse-drawn carts, laden with goods...

At the Quayside

As you stare at the jetties, wharves, and warehouses, a young Viking approaches you. He tells you his name is Erik and he has a problem. In six hours, he's due to leave on a trading voyage. There are certain items he needs, but he has no time to find them by himself. Erik's shopping list sounds a lot more interesting than you parents'! First, he needs some spare sailcloth for the voyage. You go with him to one of the shipyards. As he is buying the sailcloth, you question one of the shipbuilders.

HOW DO YOU BUILD THE SHIPS?

We cut down a tall oak tree to make the keel. Then we cut long planks of wood for the sides and shorter pieces for the supporting ribs and crossbeams. We use wooden pegs and iron rivets to join the wooden pieces together. Overlapping the side planks makes the ships very strong. We stuff animal wool and sticky tar into every joint and crack to keep out the water.

WHAT KIND OF SHIPS DO YOU BUILD?

I build fast ships for raids, exploration, and war. They're called longships. I also build passenger and cargo vessels called *knorrs*, as well as small boats for fishing and short trips around the coast.

Longships were known as "dragonships" by the Viking's enemies, because of the dragon carvings that often appeared on their prows.

WHAT POWERS THE SHIPS?

Either the wind or manpower! Every ship has a big square sail made of woven wool. When there's not enough wind, the men row with wooden oars. There's a big oar at the back end, which is used for steering the ship.

A Visit to the Weapon-Smith

Next Erik needs to buy a sword. Together you go to the weapon-smith, who finds a sword of the right length and weight for Erik. After paying for the sword, Erik gives you a list of other things he needs. He also lends you a wagon pulled by a horse to load up your purchases. Then he rushes off. But before you set off on your errands, you ask the weapon-smith some questions.

HOW IMPORTANT ARE WEAPONS TO A VIKING?

They are a Viking man's most prized possessions. There are even laws stating what weapons each man must own. In the words of a famous Viking poem: "A man should never be more than an inch from his weapons when out in the field." We're expected to be ready to fight and hunt at any time. This means I must produce the weapons I make to a very high standard.

WHAT WEAPONS MUST A VIKING HAVE?

Every man must own a sword, an axe, a spear, a bow, and three dozen arrows. I make and sell them all here. The sword is the most important of these. A good sword gets handed down from father to son, unless it's buried with its owner – that's another of our traditions.

Arrows are carried on the archer's back in a container called a quiver.

WHAT ARMOR DO YOU WEAR?

We Vikings don't wear much armor, though some chieftains wear mail shirts. Most of us rely on a round wooden shield for protection, and a helmet made of leather or iron.

Viking warriors use their wooden shields to form a protective "wall."

The Craft of the Jeweler

You need to buy some jewelry for Erik to use as bribes and gifts when he goes to foreign lands. You go to one of the many jewelers in Jorvik. Inside, you find a busy workshop filled with sounds of hammering and smoke from braziers heating molds of molten metal. After you have bought some jewelry, you chat with the jeweler.

WHAT KIND OF JEWELRY DO YOU MAKE, AND WHAT MATERIALS DO YOU USE?

Here we make brooches, pendants, necklaces, finger rings, arm rings, and earrings. We also make practical objects such as buckles, belt ends, and pins, but we always decorate them. The materials we most often use are copper, pewter, silver, gold, amber, and jet.

WHAT IS YOUR FAVORITE MATERIAL?

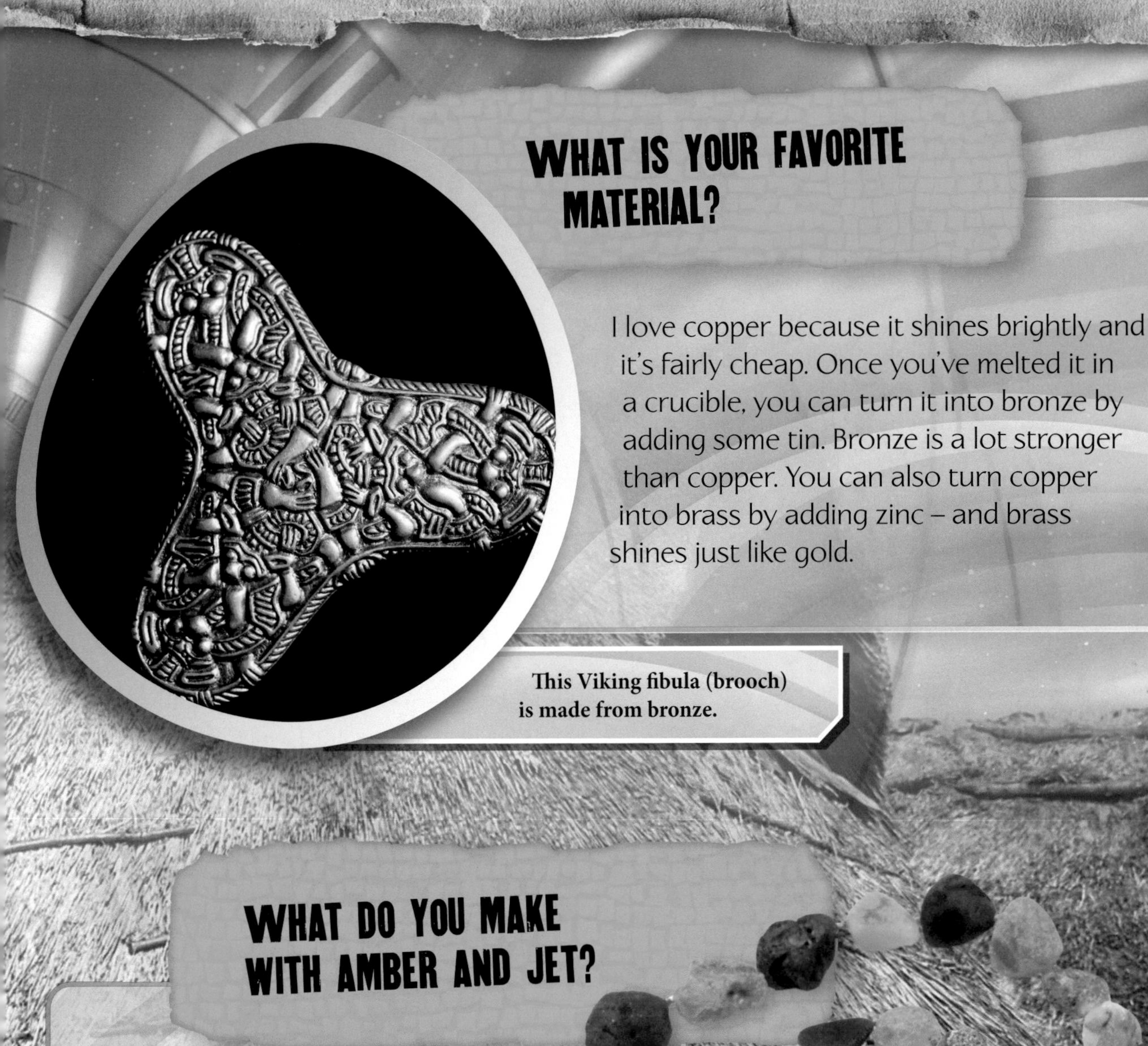

I love copper because it shines brightly and it's fairly cheap. Once you've melted it in a crucible, you can turn it into bronze by adding some tin. Bronze is a lot stronger than copper. You can also turn copper into brass by adding zinc – and brass shines just like gold.

This Viking fibula (brooch) is made from bronze.

WHAT DO YOU MAKE WITH AMBER AND JET?

We make pendants, beads, and rings. Amber is a beautiful transparent gold or yellow. We find it on the shores of the Baltic Sea. Jet is shiny and black. We get it from the coast near here. We fit it into sockets in metal jewelry and hold it in place with molten tin.

A necklace made from amber.

The Thrall

As you are leaving the jeweler, you bump into someone coming the other way. He is a thin boy dressed in a plain tunic. The boy apologizes, then introduces himself as Finn. He explains he is a thrall, or slave, and his mistress has sent him off to the farm to buy some eggs. As you are heading that way, too, you offer to accompany him. On the way, you ask Finn about his life.

COULD YOU EVER WIN YOUR FREEDOM?

If I raise enough money, I could buy my freedom, or my freedom might be purchased for me by another person. Sometimes thralls are freed by their owners as a gift, especially after long and loyal service.

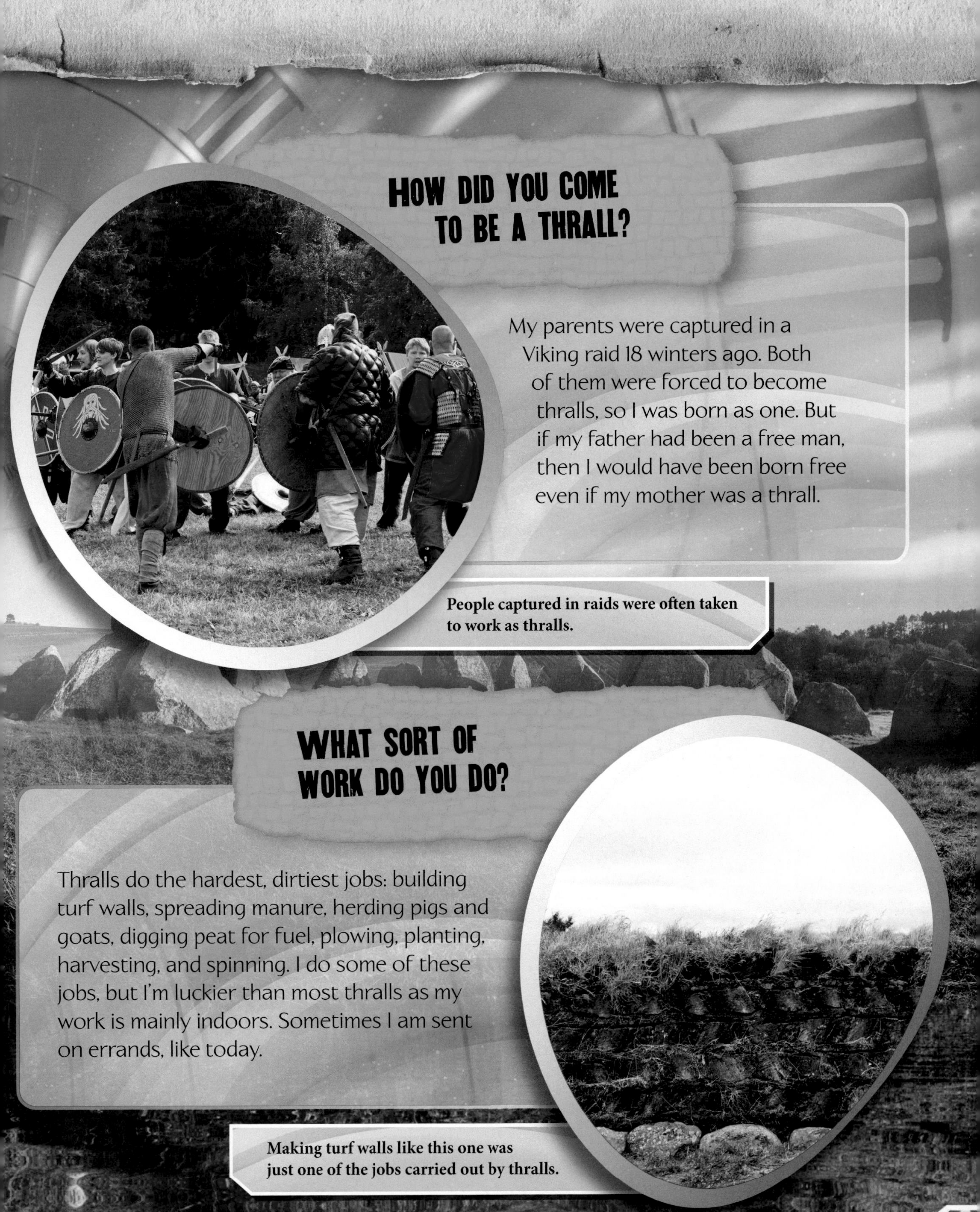

HOW DID YOU COME TO BE A THRALL?

My parents were captured in a Viking raid 18 winters ago. Both of them were forced to become thralls, so I was born as one. But if my father had been a free man, then I would have been born free even if my mother was a thrall.

People captured in raids were often taken to work as thralls.

WHAT SORT OF WORK DO YOU DO?

Thralls do the hardest, dirtiest jobs: building turf walls, spreading manure, herding pigs and goats, digging peat for fuel, plowing, planting, harvesting, and spinning. I do some of these jobs, but I'm luckier than most thralls as my work is mainly indoors. Sometimes I am sent on errands, like today.

Making turf walls like this one was just one of the jobs carried out by thralls.

Life on the Farm

Erik asked you to buy some chickens to be used as food on the voyage. You go with Finn to a busy farm on the edge of town where they keep livestock and grow crops. The farmer's wife agrees to sell you six chickens, and Finn helps you load the crates onto your wagon before bidding you farewell. Afterwards you talk with the farmer's wife.

WHAT CROPS DO YOU PRODUCE HERE?

We grow rye, oats, wheat, and barley. We grind the grain to make flour, porridge, and ale. We also grow vegetables, such as onions, beans, and cabbages.

WHAT METHODS DO YOU USE TO GROW YOUR CROPS?

To break up the soil, we plow it with an "ard" plow – a pointed wooden pole tipped with iron and dragged by horses or oxen. Then we sow the seed by throwing handfuls along the plowed furrows. When the crop is ready, we harvest it using sickles, with curved iron blades and wooden handles.

Viking farmers used sickles like this one to harvest their crops.

WHAT ANIMALS DO YOU HAVE?

Cattle, sheep, pigs, geese, and chickens. We use manure from the animals to keep the soil fertile. In the autumn, we normally slaughter some animals because there isn't enough food to keep them all through the winter.

In the Bakery

As you head back into town, disaster strikes! One of the crates containing the chickens falls off the wagon, and the chickens escape. You run after them and finally catch up with them at a bakery, where they're busy pecking at the breadcrumbs on the floor. By the time you've coaxed them back into the crate, you're quite hungry, so you buy a loaf of bread while taking the opportunity to ask the baker some questions.

HOW DO YOU BAKE YOUR BREAD?

We bake it in all shapes and sizes. Small loaves and rolls are baked in ring and oval shapes. Some bakers put the dough on round, flat pans with long handles. They bake the dough over the hot ashes of a fire. But instead of baking it like this, we have ovens to bake our bread. The ovens are domed, with clay shelves. They are heated by a wood fire.

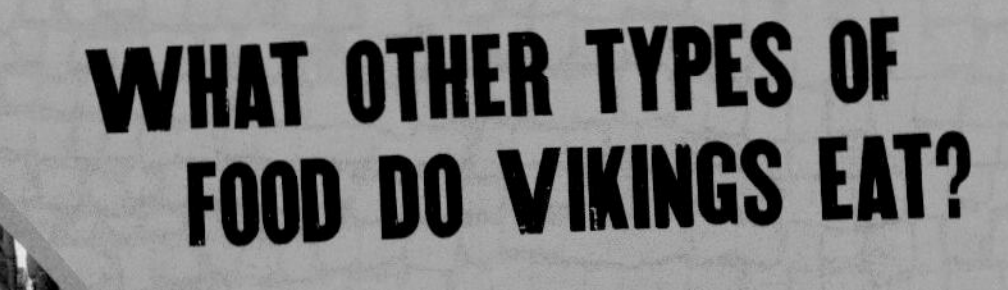

WHAT OTHER TYPES OF FOOD DO VIKINGS EAT?

We like to eat salted fish and meat. We boil seawater or seaweed to get the salt. The salt preserves the fish or meat to last us through the winter. We also preserve fish by hanging it up to dry in the wind, or putting it on racks in special huts and smoking it. We love milk, butter, and cheese, too.

Fish are hung on racks to dry in the wind.

HOW ELSE DO YOU STOP FOOD FROM GOING BAD?

We keep things cool in the pantry. It's got thick stone walls, and it's always cold in there! As well as salting meat, we also dry or smoke it to stop it from going rotten. If food does go bad, we make it tastier by adding spices to the cooking pot. The spices are very expensive because they come from faraway Eastern lands by ship.

Watching the Weaver

Erik asked you to buy him a spare tunic, so you pay a visit to a nearby weaver. She is busy spinning wool. Her walls are covered with cloth hangings to keep out the drafts. After selling you the tunic, she goes back to her spinning. As she works, she answers your questions.

HOW DO YOU PREPARE THE WOOL FOR WEAVING?

The raw wool is cleaned, then straightened, or "carded," ready for spinning. I spin the wool on a spindle and a stick called a distaff to make yarn. The yarn is dyed, usually with vegetable dyes. Red, green, yellow, purple, and brown are popular colors. Then I weave the yarn into cloth on a loom.

WHAT DO VIKING WOMEN WEAR?

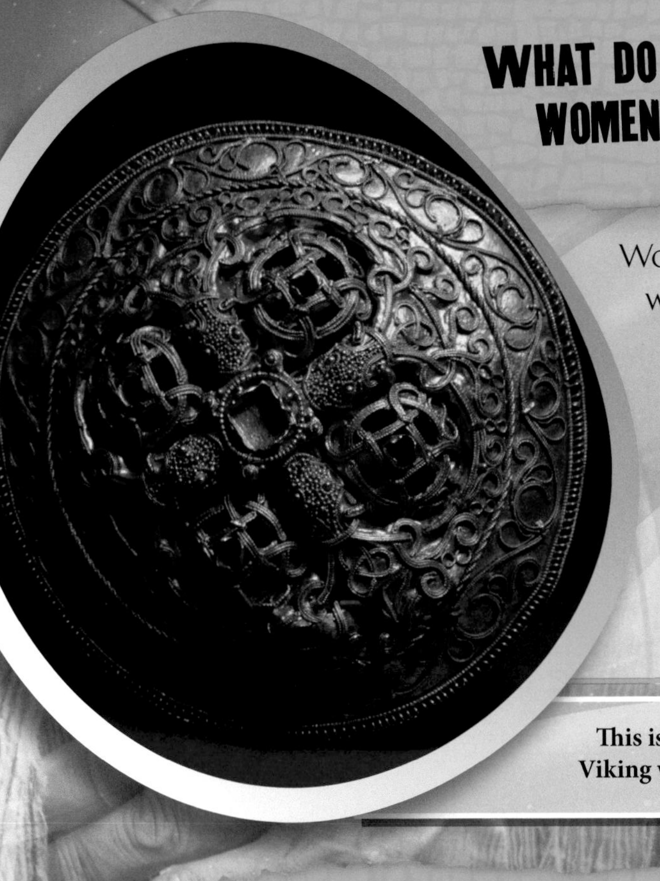

Women wear long woolen or linen shifts, which are either short-sleeved or sleeveless. Over the top, they wear a straight woolen tunic that reaches almost to the ground. It's held in place by a pair of brooches worn high on the chest. In winter, women wear stockings and linen underwear, and cloaks similar to the men's.

This is one of a pair of brooches worn by a Viking woman to fasten her woolen tunic.

WHAT CLOTHES DO VIKING MEN WEAR?

Men wear linen shirts and long pants as underwear. Over these, they wear woven tunics – red or green are the most popular colors – drawn in the middle with a leather belt. Trousers may either be baggy and short, or close-fitting and long. When it's cold, men wear fur or heavy woolen cloaks, and hats of fur, wool, or leather.

Questioning the Doctor

The weaver tells you that her daughter is ill, but she hasn't got time to take her to the doctor because she has to finish a cloak for a wealthy *jarl* – a Viking noble. You offer to go and fetch some medicine for the girl. When you get to the doctor's, you see that he has one of the best houses in town. As you talk to him, you learn that doctors have a high status in Viking society.

WHAT KIND OF INJURIES DO YOU DEAL WITH?

I treat boils, clean wounds, and stop bleeding by using hot irons. I apply herbal ointments to injuries and I set broken limbs with bandages and wooden splints. In our warlike society, I get quite a lot of practice at patching up serious injuries!

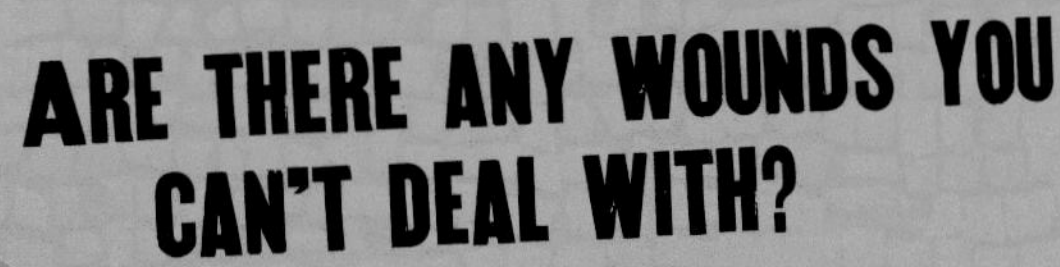

ARE THERE ANY WOUNDS YOU CAN'T DEAL WITH?

Porridge was made from oats and water.

Of course. For example, if a warrior has a spear wound in the stomach, we give him the "porridge test." First we clean and bandage the wound, then we feed him porridge flavored with onions. If, after a while, the smell of onions comes out of the wound, we know the injury has gone too deep and the patient will die. This is known as a "porridge wound."

THE VIKINGS HAVE A REPUTATION FOR NOT BEING VERY CLEAN. IS THIS TRUE?

No, it's not true! Like many Vikings, I change my underwear regularly and try to take a bath every Saturday. I always wash my hands before meals and I have a comb made from bone that I use to get rid of any lice in my hair.

A Viking bathing pool in Iceland.

Viking Games

You return to the weaver's house with some herbal medicines. The weaver's daughter is so grateful that she asks if she can offer you one of her possessions in return. You remember that Erik asked for something amusing, like a game, to help him pass the time on the long voyage. You ask the girl if she has any games she could give to Erik. She offers you a board game, and you ask her some questions about it.

WHAT IS THIS GAME?

It's called *hnefatafl*, or "king's table." The board is checkered like a chess board, but when I lay out the pieces you'll see the whites are placed in the middle and the black pieces around the sides. There are more black pieces than white. The whites have a "king" piece that must escape to the edges of the board. I love playing this game.

WHAT OTHER SPORTS AND GAMES DO YOU PLAY?

Viking boys and men enjoy swimming, wrestling, and horse racing. In the winter, I like skating with my friends on frozen rivers, or skiing over the snow. Younger children play with wooden dolls, model boats, or wooden tops. Soccer is also popular.

This wooden gaming board once had a Viking owner.

DO YOU GO TO SCHOOL?

School? You mean a place to learn things? No, we Vikings have no time for that. We must help our parents with their work. We don't have books, but we learn history, religion, and law from spoken stories and songs. When I am 15 years old, my father will choose me a husband. That's when my childhood will stop.

Viking children must help their parents with their work.

Pagans or Christians?

For protection at sea, Erik would like a crucifix amulet, so you go to the nearby church of St Olave's. It is a timber-framed building with a small, round steeple. You meet with the priest there. While he searches for a crucifix, you have an interesting conversation about Viking religious beliefs.

HOW DID THE VIKINGS COME TO BE CHRISTIANS?

People in Britain were Christians long before the Vikings arrived. At first, we Vikings thought of the Christian God as just another god alongside our pagan gods. Now many Vikings are Christians. This has happened as Viking settlers in Britain took Christian wives, and their children grew up as Christians.

WHAT CAN YOU TELL ME ABOUT THE OLD PAGAN BELIEFS?

What we know comes from folk tales passed down from parent to child. The most powerful Viking god is the one-eyed Odin, god of war, justice, death, wisdom, and poetry. But the most popular god is Thor, the god of thunder, who is particularly worshipped by seafarers.

Thor was armed with a hammer, and amulets of Thor's hammer, like this one, were popular throughout the Viking world.

ARE ALL THE VIKINGS CHRISTIAN NOW?

In Britain, the Anglo-Saxon king, Alfred of Wessex, signed a treaty with the Viking leader Guthrum in 878, in which Guthrum accepted Christianity. But many Vikings still cling to the ancient beliefs and our old pagan gods, especially in our Scandinavian homeland. You can see examples of this on some gravestones and coins, which mix symbols of the Viking gods with the crucifix of Christianity.

This Viking gravestone from the 900s shows the crucifixion of Jesus Christ.

Travel and Trade

The final item on Erik's list is a pair of folding scales. He needs the scales to weigh the coins he receives for his goods, to make sure they contain the correct amount of silver. So you go to the house of another trader who is prepared to lend Erik his spare set of scales. The six hours are nearly up, but there is just enough time to ask the trader a few questions.

WHERE DO YOU TRAVEL AND WHAT GOODS DO YOU BUY AND SELL?

We Vikings trade all over Europe, and as far east as Central Asia. We buy silver, silk, spices, wine, jewelry, glass, and pottery. In return, we sell items such as honey, tin, wheat and barley, wool, wood, iron, fur, leather, fish, and ivory from walrus tusks.

HOW DO YOU FIND YOUR WAY?

We sail close to the coast whenever possible. When out of sight of land, we look for the sun. Sailing towards sunset means we're heading west; towards sunrise means we're heading east. At night we watch the stars. Experienced seafarers can navigate by the winds and sea currents. By looking at the sea birds, or the color of the water, they can tell if land is near.

Sailing towards sunset means you are heading west.

WHAT DO YOU ENJOY MOST ABOUT YOUR JOB?

The travel. It's dangerous, but also very exciting. We Vikings are great sailors. Not only do we travel for trade, but also to explore new lands, to raid, or to settle as farmers. That's how we originally came to Britain. We've also sailed to the Faeroe Islands, Iceland, and Greenland. We've sailed into the North Atlantic and south to the Mediterranean Sea. Our ships are small, but we travel huge distances.

Back to the Present

Your six hours are over. You return to the quayside with the wagon loaded with supplies and hand them over to a grateful Erik. After saying goodbye to Erik, you find the place where you first arrived. There is a bright flash of light and the doorway reappears. You pass through it into the little room where you take off your Viking garments and change back into your original clothes. Then the door reopens and you find yourself in 21st century York. You go in search of your parents.

HOW DID THE VIKINGS COME TO YORK?

You decide to find out more about the Viking history of York. Before the arrival of the Vikings, York was founded as a Roman stronghold called Eboracum. Then it was the capital of the English kingdom of Northumbria before being captured by the Vikings in 866. The Vikings built a prosperous settlement named Jorvik. Viking farmers settled in the fertile land around the city. Jorvik also became the center of early Christianity in the north of England.

The Oseberg ship on display in Oslo, Norway.

WHAT ABOUT VIKING SHIPS?

You are intrigued by everything you heard about Viking seafaring - the distances the sailors traveled and their skill at navigation. You find out about two famous Viking ships in Norway. The Gokstad ship was uncovered in 1880, and the Oseberg ship was found in 1904. Both ships were buried in Viking funerals during the 9th century. The Gokstad ship had space for 32 oarsmen, while the Oseberg ship was slightly smaller. Both ships are now on display in a museum in Oslo.

Glossary

amulet A small piece of jewelery believed to give protection against evil, danger, or disease.

Anglo-Saxon The name given to Germanic inhabitants of England from their arrival in the 5th century up to the Norman Conquest of 1066.

brazier A container for holding lighted coals, used mainly to provide heat and light.

bribe A sum of money or a gift given to someone to persuade them to do something, or to influence a decision.

crucible A ceramic or metal container in which metals or other substances are melted or subjected to very high temperatures.

crucifix A representation of a cross with a figure of Jesus Christ on it.

distaff A stick onto which wool is wound for spinning.

ivory A hard, creamy-white substance that makes up the main part of the tusks of elephants, walruses, and narwhals.

jarl A Viking noble or chieftain.

jetty A landing stage or small pier at which boats can dock or be moored.

keel The long, central piece along the base of a ship that supports the rest of the ship's framework.

loom An apparatus for making fabric by weaving yarn or thread.

mail shirt A shirt made of metal rings or plates linked together. It was used as armor.

ointment A smooth cream used to help heal wounds.

pagan Pre-Christian religion, usually involving the worship of several gods.

parchment A stiff, flat, thin material made from the prepared skin of an animal and used as a writing surface in ancient and medieval times.

peat A brown, soil-like material found in boggy ground. It consists of partly decomposed vegetable matter and is cut and dried for use in plant cultivation and as fuel.

pewter A grey metal composed mainly of tin, with added copper, antimony, bismuth, and sometimes lead.

prow The pointed front part of a ship.

rivet A short metal pin or bolt used to hold together two sections of timber or metal.

shift A long, loose-fitting undergarment.

sickle A short-handled farming tool with a semi-circular blade, used for cutting crops.

spindle A slender rounded rod with tapered ends used in hand spinning to twist and wind thread from a mass of wool held on a distaff.

splint A strip of rigid material used for supporting a broken bone.

thrall A slave or servant.

tunic A loose garment, typically sleeveless and reaching to the wearer's knees.

wharf A quayside area to which a ship may be moored to load and unload.

yarn Spun thread used for knitting, weaving, or sewing.

For More Information

WEBSITES

www.bbc.co.uk/schools/primaryhistory/vikings/
This introduction to the Vikings has sections on family life, seafaring, towns, beliefs, trade, and much else.

www.britishmuseum.org/explore/online_tours/europe/the_vikings/the_vikings.aspx
This section of the British Museum website explores the history and culture of the Vikings through different objects.

jorvik-viking-centre.co.uk/who-were-the-vikings/
This section of the official website of the Jorvik Viking Centre looks at who the Vikings were, where they came from, how they lived, and much else.

www.pbs.org/wgbh/nova/vikings/
This website offers information about Viking villages, ships, sagas, runes (letters from the Viking alphabet), and much else. It also contains video clips.

www.timetravel-britain.com/articles/towns/jorvik.shtml
This website looks in detail at the Viking city of Jorvik (York), investigating what life was like there based on the relics archaeologists have dug up.

BOOKS

The Anglo-Saxons and Vikings (History Relived) by Cath Senker (Wayland, 2013)

Vikings (Greatest Warriors) by Philip Steele (Franklin Watts, 2013)

The Vikings (The History Detective Investigates) by Alice Harman (Wayland, 2014)

The Vikings (History from Objects) by John Malam (Wayland, 2012)

The Vikings in Britain (Tracking Down) by Moira Butterfield (Franklin Watts, 2013)

You Wouldn't Want to Be a Viking Explorer by Andrew Langley and illustrated by Dave Antram (Franklin Watts, 2013)

Index